FAVORITE MOVIE  THEMES

TRUMPET

M000159823

ISBN 0-7935-7789-6

**HAL•LEONARD®
CORPORATION**
7777 W. BLUEMOUND RD. P.O. BOX 13819 MILWAUKEE, WI 53213

Visit Hal Leonard Online at
www.halleonard.com

BACK TO THE FUTURE ◆2

from the Universal Motion Picture BACK TO THE FUTURE

By ALAN SILVESTRI

Trumpet

FORREST GUMP – MAIN TITLE
(Feather Theme)

from the Paramount Motion Picture FORREST GUMP

Trumpet

Music by
ALAN SILVESTRI

4

CHARIOTS OF FIRE ◆4

from CHARIOTS OF FIRE

Trumpet

Music
VANGEL

THE JOHN DUNBAR THEME 5
from DANCES WITH WOLVES

By JOHN BARRY

MISSION: IMPOSSIBLE THEME ◆ 6

from the Paramount Motion Picture MISSION: IMPOSSIBLE

Trumpet

By LALO SCHIFRIN

THEME FROM E.T. (THE EXTRA-TERRESTRIAL) ⬧7

from the Universal Picture E.T. (THE EXTRA–TERRESTRIAL)

Music by
JOHN WILLIAMS

STAR TREK®–THE MOTION PICTURE

Theme from the Paramount Picture STAR TREK: THE MOTION PICTURE

Trumpet

Music
JERRY GOLDSMITH

END CREDITS–APOLLO 13 ◆9

from APOLLO 13

By JAMES HORNER

THE MAN FROM SNOWY RIVER

(Main Title Theme)

from THE MAN FROM SNOWY RIVER

Trumpet

By BRUCE ROWLAND